MATEO'S
AWAKENING FROM WITHIN

DISCOVER YOUR SIX INNATE GIFTS TO SUCCEED IN LIFE!

SARA D'AMBROSIO

Copyright © 2023 Sara D'Ambrosio.

All rights reserved. This publication, or any part thereof, may not be reproduced in any form, or by any means, including electronic, photographic, or mechanical, or by any sound recording system, or by any device for storage and retrieval of information, without the written permission of the copyright owner.

Dedication

Dedicated to YOU, a beautiful soul that is looking for expansion and fuller expression. It is my wish for you to find the truth of your uniqueness.

Sincerely,

Sara D'Ambrosio

Table of Contents

Preface 1

Mateo the Dreamer 4

Mateo and the Tourists 7

Mateo Receives a Gift 10

Mateo's Explanation to His Parents 16

Mateo Calls David 19

David Mentors Mateo 21

Our 1st Gift 26

Our 2nd Gift 33

Our 3rd Gift 39

Our 4th Gift 44

Our 5th Gift 49

Our Last Gift… 58

Mateo Travels to California 63

Mateo in California… The Adventure Begins 69

Mateo Meets David's Family 72

The Secret of the Goal Card 77

Mateo's Unforgettable First Seminar 84

Healing Mateo's Heart 90

A Morning Practice That Will Change Mateo's Life 98

Mateo Discovers His Purpose in Life 103

An Unforgettable Trip is Coming to an End 109

About the Author 118

Preface

I have been taking various self-development courses for a few years now. The one I just recently completed is a year-long coaching program with Bob Proctor. If I tell you how this particular program impacted my life, you wouldn't believe me. When you are able to look around with a different perspective on life, expecting good things to happen to you, you know you are growing mentally and spiritually.

Writing a book wasn't my plan at all; actually, this is my very first book ever. The idea came to me one day while sitting in my backyard and looking at the sky. I started to recite from memory some of the material I was studying in the program and said to myself, "Why not?" For sure, it would be a challenge for me, especially because English is my second language. But I love challenges; without them, you can't grow. Minutes later, I was writing the first page of

Mateo's Awakening from Within on my tablet. The name "Mateo" came intuitively since I had to give my main character a name before I could start writing the story, and I loved it. The name kept coming back to my mind, so I decided to look up its meaning, and I found out that it means "Gift of God." I totally loved it! In English, Mateo is "Matthew".

It was amazing how the story came easily and effortlessly to me. I am from Peru, and I was in Agua Calientes (Hot Springs) when I visited Cusco. I was captivated by this colorful, mystical town with all its traditions and history. It was the perfect place for Mateo to come from in my story. Every day, during my spare time, I would write part of the story, and I got so connected with the story that sometimes I found myself with tears in my eyes.

Everything in Mateo's story is part of the teachings that I've learned and implemented every day of my life. From experience, I know the power of the techniques that are revealed in this book. I would suggest that you pay close attention to them and use them as part of your routine.

Thank you for purchasing this life-transforming book. I appreciate you, and I hope you like Mateo's story. It was written with the purpose of helping people to live a better life and sharing the powerful lessons that have impacted my life with the world.

Sincerely,

Sara D'Ambrosio

Mateo the Dreamer

Mateo was born in **Aguas Calientes**, which means "hot waters" or "hot springs." It is a popular town in the Urubamba River Valley in southeast Peru, a place known for its thermal baths and as a gateway to the nearby Inca ruins of Machu Picchu, which is about 3.7 miles away. Aguas Calientes is also known as **Machupicchu Pueblo**, and you can find hotels and restaurants that are always visited by tourists that come from all around the world to see the ruins of Machu Picchu. Some archaeologists believe that Machu Picchu was constructed as an estate for the Inca emperor Pachacuti (1438-1472).

The indigenous language of the Andes is Quechua, and for a long time, it was only a spoken language. In Quechua, Machu Picchu means "old mountain" or "old peak."

Mateo's parents, Pedro and Rosa, were poor, but they

worked very hard every day to provide all the basic needs for Mateo and his little sister, Adela. They were from a lineage of Incas with deep ties to their traditions and culture. Early in the morning, when the sun rises and roosters crow, Mateo was always ready to help feed the animals on the farm where his dad worked before going to school. He would ride his bike and speed to school. It wasn't always easy, he believes, but he believed he had no choice. He was fourteen years old, and he liked to help his family.

"Mateo!" the teacher yelled. "This is not the time to dream. Can you please tell me why you didn't finish your homework? What is your excuse this time?"

Everybody in the class laughed at him.

"Well," Mateo answered. "I am thinking about how blessed I am to have such a great teacher like you, Ms. Teresa," he answered with a smile.

Ms. Teresa had known Mateo very well since kindergarten, and she knew that he was a smart boy. She also knew how he worked hard with his dad to help his family. She knew Mateo's family very well.

Aguas Calientes is a small town, there are only a few schools, and people enjoy getting together and dancing to their traditional folklore music.

In the afternoons, Mateo worked to help clean up the waste at the sanctuary of Machu Picchu so that he could support his family with the money he earned. After his job, he liked to take some time and go to his special hidden place where he had been going for years. His Grandpa Alejandro showed him this magical place. Mateo remembered him a lot. He died a few years ago. He was an old guy, full of wisdom and very active. They used to spend lots of time together. Mateo always sat in this place and watched the sunset. It was a magical place, and he felt the energy in the air. This was his secret place where he could dream and charge his mind and body.

Mateo was a dreamer, and he knew inside of him that there was much more to learn about life. He saw his parents working hard and wanted to help them. He dreamed of a big house with lots of rooms and big windows. He thought to himself, "One day, my family and I will live in a big, beautiful house, and my parents will never have to work again."

Mateo and the Tourists

The sound of some tourists talking woke him up from his dream. Mateo approached them. He was very friendly and loved helping people. He enjoyed practicing his English with tourists.

"Hi, can I take a picture for you?" he asked them.

"Sure!" One of them replied. "Can you be so kind and take 4 pictures, please?"

Mateo loved taking pictures of tourists because some of them would tip him.

"What is your name?" they asked.

"Mateo Chavez. I live in Aguas Calientes," he replied.

"That is cool, my friend. This place is amazing!" he said, handing Mateo a $10 bill.

Mateo looked at the bill with surprise.

"Wow! $10 for a picture! This is my best tip ever! Thank you so much! This is a lot of money."

"You're very welcome, Mateo. You have been very helpful."

Mateo wanted more money and thought that if he could help them more, he could earn some extra money. So he asked, "Excuse me, if you need assistance around this town, I can help you. I know everything about this place, and I can be your tour guide. I know you won't be disappointed," Mateo told the group.

"That would be awesome! Are you available tomorrow at 8 am? We are in the Inkawasi Hotel. We can meet there. It's not far from here."

"I know that hotel," Mateo answered. "I will be there at 8 am."

"OK, Mateo! You will be our tour guide," David, the head of the group replied.

During the night, Mateo couldn't sleep as he thought about his new friends and all the money that he may bring home.

"Mateo, turn off the light, please!" Adela, his 4-year-old sister, requested.

"Ok, I'm sorry. Good night!" Mateo answered.

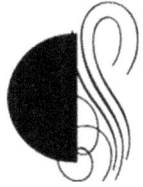

Mateo Receives a Gift

The next morning, after helping his dad, Mateo rushed to the hotel to meet the group.

"Here he is. Hi, Mateo!"

"Hi, friends! Good morning; I am ready to take you on an unforgettable tour around Aguas Calientes, my hometown," said Mateo proudly. "You will love this place. It's full of magic."

"I am sure!" A member of the group replied. "We are having such a great time here!"

During the tour, Mateo did his best to speak proper English so that they could understand him. Thank God for Ms. Teresa, his English teacher. Although some members of the group spoke Spanish, Mateo preferred to speak English to the group so he could practice it.

At 2 pm, the tour was over. The group was very grateful for Mateo; they loved his friendly personality and helpfulness.

"Mateo, you have been so helpful. Your English is very good."

"Yes!" the other guys said, "and you are such a great photographer. You must be proud to live in such a beautiful place like this."

David handed Mateo $400. Mateo was amazed. He had never had so much money in his hands, so tears started coming down his face. He felt bad about crying in front of them, but he couldn't control it.

"Mateo, what do you want to do when you are older?"

"I don't know," he answered, "but I would love to travel around the world and help people."

David, the group leader, wrote down his phone number and email address on a piece of paper and gave it to the Peruvian boy. He stared at him for a moment and said something to the boy that he would never forget.

"Mateo, I can see so much potential in you! I grew up in a very poor place, but I made my way. One thing I want you to remember is to never let anyone tell you that you can't do something."

David opened his backpack and grabbed a book, signed it, and gave it to Mateo.

"Mateo, in this book, you will find the only way to get anything you want. When I was about your age, I met a man who changed my life for good. I was a sad boy, I was always sick, and my family was very poor. I had no motivation. I thought that life was very unfair, and one day, I decided to run away from home to find more of life. I worked by cleaning cars and delivering newspapers. Many days, I went to sleep feeling hungry. One day, I was so sick with a high fever that I fell on the floor while delivering newspapers. I woke up in the hospital feeling pain in my body. I was so weak. The doctors told me that I had pneumonia, and I was lucky I was alive.

The next morning, a tall guy in a suit came to visit me. I didn't know who he was. For sure, he wasn't one of the members of my family. This guy was very educated, smelled good, and had a kind face. 'My God!' I thought. 'Maybe I am dead, and this is my guardian angel.'"

"He said to me, 'My name is Brian, and I was the person who

saw you when you collapsed on the street. I am glad you feel much better.' He asked me where my family was, and I started to cry. All these emotions that were stuck in my throat felt like a knife. I couldn't stop talking. I told this stranger what I had to do in order to survive. I told him that I had run away from home because I felt there was something else outside that poor home that I needed to find. I don't know why but I felt peace for the first time in my heart after so long. How could I feel this good in front of a complete stranger, and how was I able to open my heart to this guy I just met?

Then he replied, 'Well, David, this is the beginning of your transformation.' Brian was a rich guy, not only monetarily, but in spirit. He knew so much about spirit and personal realization that he was invited to that town for a speaking engagement. He was in his limousine when he saw me falling on the street. From that moment, this guy became my mentor. He taught me about mindset; he made me wake up and realize how powerful we are. He showed me, in a simple way, the steps to manifest anything I wanted."

Mateo scratched his head. "Manifest anything I want? Mindset? What the heck is this guy talking about?" Mateo asked himself.

"Mateo," David added, "I know this is all new for you, but I am telling you all of this not to confuse you, but to guide you. I see the potential in you, and I can feel your aura and energy. You have passion for life, and you can do so much more. You have no idea. I would like to stay longer in this beautiful place, but I have a busy schedule, and I need to go back to the USA. But I want to give you this book that will help you to understand what I am talking about. Please don't take it for granted. This book has the potential to change your life for good."

"I will read this book," Mateo replied.

"Mateo, I don't want you to read this book. I want you to study this book. Read this book every day, as much as you can, in your free time, in the morning and at night. I want you to find time to study and memorize this book. I know you don't understand now what I'm telling you, but you will if you follow my instructions."

Mateo felt the importance of David's words and promised him he would do it.

"Mateo, you have my number; call me whenever you need me. I am here for you."

"Why are you so nice to me?" Mateo asked David.

"A man did the same for me when I needed it. He saved my life. Thanks to him, I was able to change my life completely and help others. One day, if you do what I am telling you, you will do the same, and I know it," David said affirmatively. Then David and his group left.

Mateo's Explanation to His Parents

Standing in that magical place in the Andes of Peru and holding the book that David gave to him, Mateo felt like he was in a dream. He checked in his pocket, and touched his big tip, and smiled.

Looking at his watch, he realized his parents would find out he had missed school. He grabbed his backpack and rushed to Aguas Calientes.

Mateo's heart was beating faster, he opened the house door, and his parents were there waiting for him.

"Mateo, where have you been all day?" his father asked him.

"The teacher called because you didn't show up in class today, and you missed your reading test," his mom added.

Mateo, facing down and feeling embarrassed, started to talk.

"Look at us, Mateo! We want to see your eyes," his father ordered.

Mateo had never lied to his parents before, and they trusted him.

"Mom, Dad, I had a job to do."

"What kind of job!" his father yelled.

"Dad, please, let me explain."

Then he started to tell them all about the group and his special friend, David. When Mateo finished his explanation, he told his parents, "I am so sorry I missed school, but I felt this was my one chance to make some money and bring it home. I wanted to help you, Dad." He placed his hand in his pocket and took the $400 that David had given him. His parents looked at the money and Mateo and then hugged him. Mateo's parents understood his feelings.

"Hey, Son," his father said. "I don't want you to miss school anymore. And next time, I want you to trust us and tell us anything that may happen to you. Do you understand, Mateo?"

"I promise, Dad. I promise, Mom," Mateo replied.

"Good, Mateo. Now I want you to keep this money."

"But Dad, I want to give it to you."

"Thanks, Mateo, but you worked hard for it, and I believe you will use it wisely," his dad answered.

At night, when everyone was sleeping, Mateo started to read the mysterious book that his good friend had given him. He couldn't wait to start reading it.

"Mateo! Turn off your lamp, please," his sister asked him.

Mateo got his flashlight and continued reading it under the blanket. As soon as he started to read it, he realized that the name of the author was David Jones, and the picture of the author looked like his friend. He couldn't believe his eyes! His friend was the author, and he felt so blessed to meet this guy.

Mateo Calls David

A few months had passed since Mateo's first meeting with David. He had already read the book many times and kept reading it as his friend instructed him to, but he had so many questions and lots of things he didn't understand. Mateo decided to call him, so he bought a card and called his friend. To his surprise, David answered the phone.

"Hello, hi David! It's me, Mateo."

"Hi, Mateo! What a surprise! How is everything going with you?"

"Everything is fine, and thank you for your book. I have been reading it every day, as you told me."

"Very good, Mateo, you should; I was actually waiting for your call," David told Mateo.

"Did you know that I was going to call you?" Mateo asked.

"Yes, intuitively, I knew you would contact me. I am sure you have lots of questions."

"Yes, this is why I'm calling you. I have lots of questions, and I want answers. I want to change, David, and I need you to help me."

David was pleased to hear from Mateo; he knew that he was ready to learn. When the student is ready, the teacher will appear.

Mateo agreed to call David every other month at a certain time and date. His next call would be very soon, and Mateo couldn't wait.

David Mentors Mateo

It was a beautiful Friday morning, and Mateo was sitting at his classroom desk, looking through the window with a smile on his face. Then Ms. Rosita, his teacher, interrupted his dream to ask a question.

"Mateo, can you please explain to the class the difference between socialism and communism?"

Mateo looked at the board, then at the class, and finally, after a few seconds of silence, he asked, "can you explain it one more time, please? I got distracted by the beautiful butterfly that was flying around the window."

Ms. Rosita noticed something different about Mateo but wasn't sure what it was. His grades were improving in Social Studies.

"Ok, Mateo, just this once, I will repeat myself one more time. Tomorrow is the test, and I want you to study."

At the end of the class, Mateo couldn't wait to start his call with his mentor. He couldn't pay any attention in class, just thinking about it.

Finally, the time came to talk to him again. He was so happy and anxious at the same time. He biked, rushing to the internet store where he could Zoom-call his mentor.

In the video call with David…

"Hi, David. It is so nice to see you!"

"Same here, Mateo! You look great, boy; never lose that smile. I always remember you as the smiling boy from the Andes."

"No, I won't, David."

"Are you studying the book I gave you?" David asked Mateo.

"Yes, I memorized your book. When I am sad, I go back and read it again. It gives me energy; I can't explain it."

"I understand you, Mateo. It happened to me with the first book I ever read; my mentor gave it to me. It's falling apart, but I still read it and bring it with me wherever I go.

"Let me ask you this question. Do you know what the relationship is between spirit and matter?"

Mateo scratched his head and thought for a few seconds and answered. "We can't touch spirit, but matter, we can touch?"

"Yes, Mateo, great answer."

Mateo smiled, feeling proud.

"As a starting point, let's use the relationship between spirit and matter. Now, what do I mean by that? I'm talking about the thoughts that flow into your consciousness. Let's use brick as an example of a physical element. There are two completely different elements of life; thought is nonphysical, and brick is physical. But there are natural oppositions between the two; we refer to one as living spirit and the other as dead matter.

Mateo, we do live through our senses. We go by what we hear, see, smell, taste, and touch, and this is how it is. Nothing is wrong with that, but the error is when we judge just by external appearances.

The world must wake up and realize that we live in a limited world if we live by our senses alone. Mateo, if you study what I am telling you, your life will change dramatically; you will feel as if you are living in a dark room and someone opens the door. This door will take you to infinite possibilities.

In my book, you read about our creative faculties; those are our gifts from heaven, from God, from the universe, from infinite intelligence, or whatever you want to call it. But no other creature on this marvelous planet has them other than humans.

You see, Mateo, animals have instincts. We don't have instinct, but we have creative faculties.

Now, that's a beautiful thing to know; we can create our world, we've been given creative tools, and we are creative beings. Just talking about it and thinking that we can create our own world gives me a feeling of gratitude.

Do you understand what I'm saying?

Why is it that it looks like a bad economy to a lot of people? Still, there are people who are having huge wins while other people are losing in the same marketplace and in the same business. So, it's not in the marketplace or the business; the result is in our thoughts, inside each of us. We make our own economy, Mateo.

In the following months, I will explain in detail about our creative faculties. From now on, let's call them "Our Gifts". You will realize that inside of you lives a genie, a genie with superpowers, and you can have anything you want just by using your gifts in the proper way."

Mateo was thrilled; he was so amazed by what he was discovering. He made the decision right away that he would study these materials for the rest of his life. He wanted to know more about our gifts and the best way to use them. He knew something in him was changing. He felt different, but he didn't know what it was.

Our 1st Gift

"The imagination is literally the workshop wherein are fashioned all plans created by man. The impulse, the DESIRE, is given shape, form, and ACTION through the aid of the imaginative faculty of the mind. It has been said that man can create anything which he can imagine."

— **Napoleon Hill,** Think and Grow Rich

"Mateo, there are six gifts that were given to us. As I told you before, these gifts separate us from all the animal kingdoms because by using them, we can change our world. I am going to start with one of the most important. This gift is *Imagination*. We used this gift when we were kids. We thought of ourselves as singers, policemen, and presidents; our imagination was in high gear. We lived in the land of a free imagination, but then, as we start getting older, our imagination gets blurred. Even though we still have this gift within us, we use it in the wrong way, and most of the time, we use it against ourselves.

We must realize that every single thing we can see has been created twice. First, it was a thought before it became a thing."

This statement made Mateo realize why he was living in poverty. His parents were good people, but they were always saving money in case something bad happened. He started realizing that all that was lacking around him started as a thought.

"Mateo, we're going to talk now about how you can use this great faculty to imagine yourself into any possible future you would like. There are an infinite number of possible futures, but it's up to you how you want to see yourself. I want you to allow yourself to imagine and think about what type of life you would like to have. What clothing are you wearing? Where do you live? Do you travel? Are you helping others? Just imagine and don't put any restrictions; just let your imagination fly. Let's put it this way. If you knew that you could have anything you wanted by just asking, what would you ask? What would you love?

I have studied with many mentors in my life, and one important thing that I know for a fact is that we can create anything that we can imagine. And I am proof of that. When I started to study these materials, I had less than zero, and I didn't believe in myself. My parents died when I was just a kid, and my grandparents took care of me. They were very poor, and they always struggled to provide me with basic necessities.

I lived in abject poverty until I found the guy who woke me up from my illusion. He was the flashlight in the dark room I was in. And even though I didn't believe in myself, I knew he did, and that changed everything for me."

David started to explain that there are two forms of imagination. One is known as synthetic imagination, and the other is creative imagination.

He explained that the synthetic imagination creates nothing; it just arranges old concepts and ideas into new combinations. For example, picture an iron. At first, it used coal, and they were very heavy. Then, someone thought about using electricity and a lighter material instead of coal. Time passed, and the iron was modified to the one we now have with different features, such as electricity-saving, different settings for different types of fabrics, etc. We can take anything we have and improve upon it through the use of synthetic imagination.

He went on to explain that creative imagination is when a man has direct communication with infinite intelligence, God, formless substance, etc.

Mateo got chills just imagining that he was able to connect to God and bring his wishes to life. When you use your creative imagination, you can find ideas, ways, and solutions to your problems that you never thought were possible. He used the Wright brothers as an example. They used their creative imagination, and they introduced us to a new world. They invented what no one thought was possible and created the first flying machine. Their first flight stayed in the air for 12 seconds.

All these new ideas were so new for Mateo, but he wanted to know more. He was like a thirsty sponge wanting to get all the information, and he couldn't wait. He knew a whole new door was opened.

"Mateo, I have to go to a meeting, but this is what I want you to do these upcoming months before our next meeting. I want you to read the chapter on imagination over and over. Remember, repetition is the key. Read it until you see yourself doing it.

As an exercise on this topic, I want you to grab a piece of paper and write down how you want your life to be. Write everything in detail. Let me ask you this; if you had a genie in front of you, and you knew that this genie would give you anything you wanted, what would it be? Do not write your wishes based on circumstances; just ask yourself, 'What would I love?'

Whenever you feel off track, go back to your paper and read about your dream life. Get involved emotionally with it, and don't tell anyone about it. Don't ask why. Just do it the way I am telling you for one month. I will explain it to you in our next conversation. It was a pleasure to serve you, Mateo. I will write you an email and let you know the date for our next meeting."

A few weeks later…

As the next meeting with his mentor approached, Mateo prepared questions for him. For sure, he had lots of questions. He was eager to learn; he wanted to learn more and more. He was practicing his imagination as much as he could. He saw himself many times in his imagination, walking in his new home and having conversations with his family next to the fireplace. He also had a pet named Milo; he was a cute toy poodle. Mateo always dreamed of a small toy poodle. When he was 5, his mother brought home a small poodle. The owner, Mrs. Duncan, was traveling for a few days with her family, and Mateo's mom, who was at that time working for her as a housekeeper, took the job of taking care of Milo for a few days. Those days were Mateo's best days. He was the one in the family taking care of Milo. At night, when everyone was sleeping, Mateo would bring him under his blanket and snuggle with his fluffy friend. Mateo cried for days when Milo was picked up. He would never forget Milo, his fluffy friend.

On the morning of the Zoom call, Mateo was happy; he felt so much gratitude for being able to call David, his mentor. He was an interesting guy and famous in the self-development field. He was a New York Times best-selling author. Mateo was still in shock that he had met him and even more that he was his mentor. He was determined to do everything David would tell him to do.

"Hi, Mateo! Sorry, I am a little late for the call. It was because I had a situation at home. How are you doing today?"

"I am doing great! Thank you for asking. I hope everything is good in your home."

"Oh yes! We saw a beautiful blue bird enter through one of the windows in our family room, and she was flying around the house, trying to find a way out. So my family and I opened all the windows and doors for the bird to escape. She finally did; it was so special seeing the bird free again, back where she belonged. I have a nice connection with blue birds. Back when I was in my teens, as I was praying, looking at the sky, and crying for answers, one blue bird came and stood on a tree close to where I was. For some reason, I felt that it was God telling me that he was right there with me and that I was never alone. Believe it or not, since then, I started seeing more and more blue birds, not just in my sad moments but also in my happy ones. If I don't see them, I can hear them, even on my birthday.

Our 2nd Gift

"The intuitive mind is a sacred gift."

- Albert Einstein

"There is only one mind, one unlimited, overflowing, all-powerful, all-knowing mind, and we are the expression of this mind. When we think, we think in pictures. If I ask you to think of a soccer ball, a picture of a soccer ball will show up in your mind. If I ask you to think of your mind, a picture of a brain will probably show up in your mind, but your mind is not in your brain; your mind is in every part, in every cell in your body. So to have a clear picture of the mind, I want you to use your imagination and see a big circle representing your head connected by a vertical line to a small circle; the small circle represents your body.

Now, Mateo, I want you to divide the big circle into two parts, so drive a horizontal line in the middle of the big circle, and let's call the top part your conscious mind and the bottom of the circle, we will call it the subconscious mind. Now imagine your senses (sight, sound, smell, taste, and touch). They are like antennas hooked up to the top (conscious mind). This top part is also referred to as the educated mind, objective mind, etc. The outside world feeds information into the conscious mind through these antennas, or sensory factors. Now the bottom half of this big circle (the subconscious mind) is also referred to as the subjective mind, universal or infinite intelligence, etc.

The difference between these two minds is that the conscious mind can accept or reject ideas, and the subconscious mind, on the other hand, will accept everything as true. These two minds communicate with each other, and whatever idea the conscious mind impresses upon the subconscious will affect your whole body. The body is an instrument of the mind. Pay attention, Mateo; the subconscious mind can communicate to the conscious mind through a mental faculty called 'INTUITION'. This is another one of our gifts.

These gifts are our mental muscles, and the way we make

them strong is by exercising them.

We usually live hooked up to the tv, the news, and external circumstances that our senses tell us. We believe in the quote, "I believe it when I see it." We must see it first in our minds. How we do that is by using our creative faculties.

It's so amazing to know that we are connected with universal intelligence. We can ask questions and get the answers. Remember, for any question, there must be an answer. When you ask a question, know that you are connected to the source, to infinite intelligence, and you have to pay attention to the hunches in the inspired inside. If you feel that you have to contact a person, do it! If you feel that you shouldn't accept that job that apparently looks amazing, don't accept it. Even though your senses are telling you to do the opposite, you have to trust that inner voice that is talking to you. Do not let the outside world mess everything up.

One important way to develop intuition is through the practice of meditation or quiet time. When your mind is relaxed and quiet, it is open to receive messages from the universe that is all-powerful and all-knowing, and this power is within you. When you are in a hurry, when you fear and worry, you are cutting the wires that connect you to the source. Practice calming your mind every day, practice breathing exercises, and you will see how your intuition will improve. Remember, Mateo, when you ask a question, open your mind and be available to receive the answer.

I hope that I was able to easily teach you about this great creative faculty and that you understand it."

"Yes!" Mateo answered. "We are connected with infinite intelligence, and we always get our answers."

"Yes, Mateo, you are totally right. We humans are sometimes so busy with our daily commitments that we don't allow infinite intelligence to flow freely through us. We are too busy to stop, breathe, meditate, and notice what the universe wants to tell us. Instead, we ask our friends, family, and neighbors questions, looking for answers when the answer is already here within us."

After the meeting with his mentor, Mateo couldn't wait to get to his special place in the mountains of Machu Picchu. He always enjoyed sitting on a rock and just getting the energy from that special place. He loved to look at the mountains and the ruins where his ancestors lived for so many years. This time, he closed his eyes and asked God for guidance. And he felt so much peace and joy that he knew he was going in the right direction. He felt a profound feeling that he was being guided.

Within weeks of practicing meditation and going within, Mateo started to develop a strong intuition. He was more relaxed and was able to meditate for longer periods of time. He had a beautiful dream about finding a beautiful, blue feather, and he felt so happy in his dream. When he woke up, he tried to understand it. Maybe it was related to the story of the blue bird his friend had told him.

One morning, Mateo was preparing for the Inti Raymi Festival, which is a festival of the sun celebrated every year precisely during the winter solstice on JUNE 24. This festival is one of the most important events in Cusco (the capital of the Inca empire), and it attracts thousands of visitors from all over the world. Mateo's friend, Walter, was going to pick them up in his truck to take them where the preparations were taking place in Cusco. Mateo felt a strong feeling about not going with him, something he couldn't explain. But as he understood more about intuition, Mateo decided to feign that he got a strong stomach ache and asked his family if they could go home with him to take some medicine. Mateo's family decided to go home with Mateo and take a bus instead. Hours later, the family was informed that Mr. Walter was in the hospital with multiple injuries. He had an accident in his truck on the way to the fest.

Mateo couldn't believe it. He started to shake and realized the power of following your intuition and being connected to infinite intelligence. He prayed for Mr. Walter and thanked God for that protection.

As the meeting with his mentor was coming soon, he started to feel impatient again. He had to tell his friend about his experience with intuition and have all his questions written down.

Finally, the day to see his mentor came again, and Mateo was so excited to see him. He started to tell him what he experienced with intuition and about his meditation practices.

David was pleased to listen to Mateo and see him growing in spirit.

Our 3rd Gift

"The next gift, Mateo, is a powerful tool at our service. It is a tool that many people use incorrectly. You see, Mateo, many people think that willpower is forcing things using the mind, but only the people who are using this gift from the universe correctly are winning big. With the imagination, the special gift we talked about before, we can form mental pictures and images in our mind; the will gives you the ability to hold this image in your mind. It doesn't matter what is happening in the outside world; you will concentrate on that picture firmly in your mind. It is like opening a passage that takes your images to the subconscious mind or infinite intelligence. I just feel so grateful right now for this marvelous gift. It is really amazing how everything flows so perfectly and beautifully in the universe.

The will is the part of your personality that gives you the ability to concentrate."

"But…" Mateo interrupted. "How can we concentrate?"

"Great question, Mateo; there are many techniques to help you concentrate. The most common and effective ones are the candle flame and the dot on the wall. With the first one, you need to concentrate on a candle flame; you can repeat the phrase 'candle flame, candle flame, …' if you prefer to use a candle while concentrating on it. Some people find that repeating 'candle flame' helps them to focus on the flame. But it's up to you. I am sure that with the practice and use of this method, it will be easier and easier to focus, so you won't need to repeat anything.

The second method is very popular; you just draw a small dot on the wall in front of your chair and concentrate on this dot as much as you can. At the beginning, you should probably concentrate for a few seconds. Soon, different thoughts will come up, but you should let them go and then go back to the dot; it's all part of the training. But if you persist and keep your focus on the dot, you will soon become one with the dot. Do it for a few minutes a day, and you will see how your willpower improves.

When you force your willpower, you may only do it for a short period of time. For example, you say to yourself, 'I am going to stop drinking soda,' but if your power is weak, it won't last. You have to allow for this real power to move through you by holding the image of what you want in a concentrated way.

My goodness, Mateo, if you do the exercises that I told you, and you practice your willpower, you will be able to move mountains. Maybe you think I'm exaggerating, but the only way you'll know it's true is by doing it and being your own judge."

Mateo was so excited about what his mentor revealed to him that after his Zoom call, he rushed to his home to draw a dot on the wall and practice this technique.

When he started to do it, he realized how difficult it was to concentrate on the dot. Different thoughts would come to his mind over and over again, but he was determined to master it. He wouldn't give up; he knew that this technique, although simple, was not easy to do, but he knew it was going to be a game changer in his life. Mateo knew that his mind was similar to a monkey in a cage; it was everywhere.

This bad habit caused him lots of trouble, especially at school. So he decided that he would dedicate some time to doing this exercise every day.

A few months had passed since the first meeting with his mentor, and Mateo was more and more involved in developing his mental gifts. He was feeling different. He was enjoying the use of them and noticed that things were changing inside of him, not around him yet, but for sure inside of him.

In the following meeting with his mentor, Mateo felt so at peace, He was excited about seeing him again, but he felt relaxed.

"Hi, Mateo! So nice to see you always on time; you have such a great attitude. The way you look and talk is changing for the better. I don't mean that you didn't look good before, but you really look sharp. Do you feel different, Mateo?"

"I do! Your book says that to change the world outside of you, you must change the world inside of yourself. When I read it, it gave me the chills. I knew right away that it was true, so I decided to improve my appearance. I didn't buy new clothes; I don't have the money yet. But my clothes are now ironed and have no holes. I also started to comb my hair and use hair gel. Lol, my family is thrilled to see this; even people at school are taken aback. They make fun of me. They think I have a girlfriend, but it's not true. I don't care about girls."

David started laughing with Mateo and was so proud of him. He felt so connected to this boy and really enjoyed his video calls.

Our 4th Gift

"Mateo, what do you understand about memory?" David asked.

"It's another gift?" Mateo answered.

"Yes, you are right, Mateo. Memory is another one of our gifts, and not many people understand the power of this mental faculty. I often hear people saying that they don't have a good memory, but the truth is that everyone has a perfect memory."

Mateo interrupted to say, "I am confused; sometimes I have trouble in school because I forget to do my homework, and I also get in trouble at home because I forget to do things my parents ask me to do."

"Mateo, you have a perfect memory, but your memory is

weak now. You just need to exercise it. Remember, like the other creative faculties, they all are our mental muscles, and in order for them to get stronger, you need to exercise them. Does that make sense?"

"Totally," Mateo answered.

"There is perfection in every molecule of our being. We are perfect; we are the highest form of creation. We have a perfect memory, but no one tells us how to use it, not in school or our home, so we never learn. The trick is to bring that perfection to the surface, and the only way we know, Mateo, is through study. There is no other way. Every time you become more aware of who you really are and the perfection within you, you will see it in your results and in your outside world.

Memory is developed through association, not just association, but ridiculous association.

When you start using this technique, you will probably feel silly, but go ahead and enjoy being silly because that is how you are going to develop your memory. Your brain loves fun; the stronger you make the connections, the longer you will remember the information. So we have to put the information in our brain the way the brain likes to have it.

I will give you an example. Let's say you need to remember to call your mom this afternoon at 4 o'clock to remind her to take her medication, and then you need to go to the grocery store to buy some bananas and milk; how are you going to remember all this?"

"You write it out?" Mateo answered.

"Funny!" David answered. "If you want to challenge yourself, you better try this technique. It is actually very simple. In fact, there are different techniques, and this is just one of them. Of course, the images will be different for different people. You have to use your own images.

So, in order to remember all this, imagine your mom wearing a t-shirt with a big number 4, holding her medication next to the milk section in your grocery store, sitting on a banana."

Mateo laughed.

"Yes, Mateo, I know it's silly, but it works. Try it out. I would suggest you practice this. There are many books out there on the subject. You can remember names, numbers, dates, anything. I will give you some techniques that I wrote for you. At the end of our conversation, I want you to print them, and I want you to do the different exercises. You will be amazed at how your memory will improve.

Memory is something invaluable; when you have a good memory, your confidence improves. I would suggest that you study every day for at least an hour. Create a routine where you have time to study. In a very short time, you are going to like yourself much better. You will discover, without a doubt, that you possess everything you need to create everything you want, Mateo."

Mateo was fascinated with his conversation with David. He gained so much wisdom every time this man opened his mouth.

Mateo spent so much time doing the memory exercises; he didn't notice that he was really improving his own.

He would ask his classmates at school to write 20 different objects on the chalkboard. He was then able to look at them for a short time, turn around, and name them. Mateo's classmates were amazed by his memory. His teachers were so fascinated with this new Mateo that they started asking him what he was doing.

As the anniversary of the school approached, Mateo was asked to do a recital. He did not like recitals at school. He thought that he wasn't that talented, but this time, he was happy to be part of it. Mateo was asked to memorize a long poem by Miguel de Cervantes, the creator of Don Quixote, the most famous figure in Spanish literature. In past years, he would never accept this challenge, but now it was different. He was happy and proud to do it.

In the next few days, as the school recital was approaching, Mateo started having second thoughts about doing the recital. He was close to memorizing the poem but was struggling to recite it; for some reason, he started getting nervous. He was happy that the meeting with his mentor was coming soon. Mateo was sure David would give him some techniques to feel more confident.

Our 5th Gift

"Thinking is the hardest work there is, which is probably the reason why so few engage in it."

- Henry Ford

In the next meeting with his mentor, Mateo shared all his new adventures regarding memory and his feelings about the recital that was coming soon. He told David about how he was improving his memory, and all that he was able to do in his class, and all the people that wanted to know more about this technique. He also shared his fear about going on stage to recite a poem.

David replied, "Something that I learned in my first years of studying these materials is that we don't need to try hard to get the result that we want. You see, when I started my career, I struggled to make things happen. I thought that in order to succeed, I had to put in more hours of work and try harder.

Mateo, trying harder is not the answer. You have to allow things to happen. When you are in harmony with the laws of the universe, when you are calm and have faith, this will come naturally. You will get there through understanding, and the only way you will understand is by studying.

Listen to this. Bugs' wings are made of cuticles, which are the world's strongest and second most common natural material. A chameleon's eyes can swivel 180 degrees if they need to, and rats have an incredibly strong sense of smell. So imagine how much more infinite intelligence can do for a reasoning, rational being with a mind that works with life principles.

You have the power to tune in with infinite intelligence anytime you want. It is flowing to and through your body all the time, and you make it positive or negative with your thoughts. Use your reasoning factor to be aware of your feelings and ask yourself, 'What am I feeling right now?' If you are feeling worried, sad, upset, anxious, or depressed, you can change it! Use your reason and understand that you are the only one who can change it, just by changing the frequency of your thoughts.

It's the same when you are watching the news and you don't like what you see; you don't force that frequency to change; you just change the channel.

An excellent way to change the frequency that you are in is as simple as a breathing exercise. Breathing deeply, you inhale and hold your breath for about 3 seconds, then exhale, imagining that all the stress, the worry, and all that your body doesn't need is expelled from your body. Keep doing this as much as you need until you feel better. When I have more time, I do meditation. I just close my eyes and concentrate on my breathing, and I visualize a beautiful light going around my body, giving me energy and love.

Mateo, ask yourself, 'Why am I nervous about the fest? Is it because I didn't memorize the whole poem? Is it because I am afraid to forget what I have memorized? Or because I am afraid of what people will think about me if I don't perform well?'"

"I don't know. All of the above." Mateo answered.

"Mateo, from now until the fest, during your free time, I want you to visualize feeling great in front of the audience;

visualize everyone clapping at the end of your recital. See it and feel it. See the smiling faces of the audience and your parents feeling proud.

I remember the first time I had to talk in front of an audience. I felt my hands sweating and my heartbeat raising. I wanted to run away, but thank God, I suddenly remembered what my mentor had told me once. You get nervous because you are thinking about what the audience is going to think about you; instead, focus on giving them your best and transmitting what you want to teach them in the best way possible. It felt so good as soon as I remembered that. My body relaxed, and I concentrated just on serving my audience and giving them the best of me.

I want you to do your recital and give the best of yourself. Everything is energy; words are energy; transmit that beautiful energy that you have to your audience. Don't think about forgetting your lines, but if you do, just keep going. You never fail, Mateo, if you keep going and give your best. It's a beautiful experience.

When we are moving towards the manifestation of our dreams, we use our reasoning factor to know that what our senses are telling us is just the result of previous thinking. This could be the house where we live, the people around us, the addictions we may have, or what we did or didn't do. But all these are the feedback of previous thinking. Remember this; it's very important. Your destiny is not determined by your history without your permission.

Start using your reasoning right now, and use your amazing gifts to switch your current situation. I know you're doing it. I can feel your vibration rising and rising. Listen to this poem written by Walter D. Wintle: 'Life's battles don't always go to the stronger or faster man, but sooner or later, the person who wins is the one who thinks he can!'

Use your reasoning factor to change your perception of things. In our next meeting, perception is going to be our topic."

Mateo felt his worries dispelling; he felt lighter and happy again. His mentor was miles and miles away, but he felt his energy and thought he was so blessed to have a mentor in his life.

The night of Mateo's recital finally came. It was the first time in Mateo's life that he would be in front of an audience. He felt nervous but confident. He knew his lines and remembered his mentor's last conversation. When the time came, Mateo stood in front of the audience and started his recital with the feeling of transmitting to them what the author of the poem wanted to transmit. At the end, everyone was in silence; he looked at his mom sitting in the front row. With tears in her eyes, She ran to Mateo and hugged him. All of a sudden, everyone stood up and clapped so loud that the auditorium was filled with beautiful energy. Mateo won an award for the best poem performance. It was an experience that he will never forget. He was happy that he changed his thinking regarding being in front of an audience.

Some months had passed since Mateo was introduced to self-realization materials. Mateos's life was changing for the better, and he was able to teach these materials to his family. He felt happier in spirit and hungry for more information. One day after school, he felt an urgent need to go to the Inkawasi Hotel, where his mentor David used to be. This is a 5-star hotel close to the Machu Picchu ruins.

"Hi, how can I help you?" a lady at the front desk asked Mateo.

"Hi, I would like to talk to the manager of this hotel, please."

"I'm sorry, but the manager is in a meeting. Would you like to leave a message and your phone number so he can contact you later?"

Mateo didn't have a phone; he had been using the internet store close to his home for his video calls with his mentor.

"Ok, I prefer to come back another time," Mateo replied.

As he was leaving the hotel, he heard a strong voice calling his name. He turned to see who was calling, and to his surprise, it was one of the group members that was with David months ago when Mateo first met his mentor.

"Here he is, my favorite tour guide. How are you, Mateo? It is so nice to see you. What are you doing here?"

"Hi, Walter! Same here. I didn't expect to see you here. When did you come back? Are you visiting the ruins again?" Mateo asked Walter.

"No, Mateo, I live here. This is my hotel; I am the owner." Mateo couldn't believe what he was hearing.

"I didn't know you were the owner. I live close to this place, but I've never seen you before."

"Well," Walter replied, "I used to live in California, but just recently, I decided to move here and live in my hotel while taking care of my business."

"What are you doing here, Mateo?"

"I wanted to talk to the manager. I am looking for a part-time job."

"Mateo, don't look anywhere else; I would like to have you on my team. You are bilingual, smart, and friendly. Actually, I am in need of a server for our VIP restaurant. Are you interested in the position?"

"Of course! I am a fast learner, and I promise I will give my 100%."

"I am sure you will, Mateo. Now, why don't you join me for dinner? I would like to know more about you. Are you hungry?"

"Yes, I am, Mr. Walter."

"Why 'Mr.'?"

"You are my boss now."

"Lol. Please, Mateo. To you, I am Walter."

That night at home, Mateo still couldn't believe what had happened during the day. He was amazed by the coincidence that Walter, his mentor's friend, was the owner of the hotel he wanted to work at. "But was it really a coincidence? he asked himself. He enjoyed the dinner with Walter and talking about David; it was like a dream. He was so ready to start working and couldn't wait for his first day of job training.

Our Last Gift...

"Hi, Mateo. Sorry I wasn't able to have our call last month; I was traveling around Europe, having different seminars. Going from place to place, I had to adjust to the new schedule. I was very busy, but I enjoyed every moment in Europe. I really love my job. It's so rewarding.

Thank you for understanding. Now tell me. What is going on with you? I can feel some sadness in you. Is everything ok?"

Mateo was amazed by David's intuition.

"My mom fell off a chair trying to put up some curtains, but she slipped. She twisted her ankle, and thank God she didn't have a concussion. She is now at home, but she is in pain. I feel so bad for her; I don't know what to do to help her. She says that she is fine, but I know she is in pain."

"Sorry to hear that, Mateo. I know it is sad when someone we love is not feeling well, but we can send them good energy. Visualize your mom with white light around her and green light in the part of the affected area. Green light is a healing light. Coincidentally, today, we will study perception, which is one of our creative faculties. I'm sure that at the end of our study, you will be able to see what happened to your mom in a different way."

"Wow! So many coincidences have happened these days. I went looking for a job at the Inkawasi Hotel, where you were hosting, and you won't believe who was there."

"Let me guess," answered David, "you saw Walter?"

"How did you know that?"

"Well, Walter and I are good friends. We met in California during a conference, and since then, we have become good friends. I am in touch with him, and he told me the good news about your new job as a waiter in his hotel."

"Yes, David, what a coincidence that I went to look for a job in his hotel."

"Well, the reality is that there are no coincidences, Mateo; you will understand when you study more in-depth about the laws of the universe. Everything flows in a precise order.

As you are more and more connected to your inner self, you are more in harmony with the universe and what you are seeing now; those 'coincidences' are just the manifestation of your connection with infinite intelligence."

Mateo enjoyed the meetings with his mentor; David always had the right words to elevate Mateo's energy and make him feel good.

"Mateo, use this situation about your mom to change your perception in your favor. You are going to help her in a big way if you do that rather than feeling sorry for her. For example, now that your mom is not able to move around, you can spend more time with her and talk about what you are learning. Give her the book I gave you.

Sometimes, we don't understand why things happen. We think something is bad, but we can change our perception of what is happening. Maybe your mom needed this time for herself, and now she can study while she is recovering. What a great opportunity!

I remember one day, I met a guy who told me his story about boarding a plane. He started getting sick before the plane took off, and he couldn't fly. He was very upset because he had an important meeting to attend. Guess what happened?

The plane crashed in the ocean 40 minutes after taking off. There were no survivors. This incident impacted his life in many ways. He realized the power of perception. When something that seems to be bad happens to me, I always tell myself… but maybe it isn't. And I change my perception right away.

I thought that the reason for my circumstances, the lack of money and the hard work I had to do when I was a kid was my parents' fault because they abandoned me. I blamed them, my grandparents, and the universe for what was happening in my life. I was focusing on all the reasons for why my life was so bad. I was constantly putting myself down until my mentor woke me up and made me think for the first time. I still remember so clearly when he looked me straight in the eyes and told me, '"If you would change your point of view and look at yourself in a different way, your life would be so much different.'

You have a perception problem. Mateo, you first need to understand who you really are. You are God's highest form of creation, you can do anything you want, and you have higher faculties. You need to start using them, and in a relatively short period of time, you will look back and be amazed at how much your life has changed."

"I have to admit that I didn't believe that I could change my life," David added, "but I could feel that my mentor believed in me, and that changed my world. I started doing everything this guy asked me to do."

"Thanks for your guidance, David; I am feeling much better for sure."

"My pleasure, Mateo! I believe that the incident with your mom is meant to bring more happiness for her and for the family. What a great example of perception, our last gift to study."

The months passed, and Mateo was involved more and more in practicing his creative faculties; he promised his mentor that he would, and he was changing his life. David promised him that he would be in contact very soon after his long trip to Asia had ended. Mateo, in the meantime, concentrated on his studies and his new job in the restaurant.

Mateo Travels to California

It was the 27th of January, and Mateo was turning 15. He loved his birthdays because his mom always made a special, dark chocolate-flavored cake and his favorite lunch. He never had much, but he realized he was blessed for all the love that surrounded him. Mateo was relieved when he found out that wanting more was not a bad thing because he really wanted to have so much more, but he also wanted to give more and help people.

Mateo couldn't fall asleep the night before; the smell of his favorite cake filled up the house. In the morning, his family woke him up singing a birthday song, and his mom, holding the cake, asked Mateo to make a wish and blow out the candles. Mateo said to himself, "I want to be rich and help people," and then blew out the candles.

That afternoon, his family received a mystery package with no sender identified. But it had a note that read, "Happy Birthday, Mateo! Enjoy your special day. Love, your friend."

Mateo's parents knew about David. Mateo always shared with them what he was learning, and they knew about his Zoom calls with his mentor. They were pleased to see Mateo growing, not just in size, but spiritually as well.

"Mateo! Mateo! Come here now, please! There is one more surprise!"

Mateo rushed, smiling. "Yes! I am here! I'm coming." When Mateo entered the room, he saw a big box wrapped in green paper with a big, gold bowl.

"Wow!!! What is this? Open it, Mateo," his dad asked him.

Mateo read the note, and his heart started beating faster. He rushed to open the box, and to his surprise, there was another smaller box inside. Mateo smiled. He knew his friend's sense of humor. He opened the next box and the next one and finally got to the last one.

"Open it, Mateo!" His mom yelled.

His hands were sweating; he loved the cute, little box so much that he didn't want to damage it. When he opened it, he saw something he couldn't imagine. It was a ticket to California for a whole month. His name was on the ticket. He thought he was dreaming. He didn't say a word for a while; he was just staring at the ticket.

"Mateo! Are you ok, honey?" his mother asked him.

Mateo turned back to his family, and he had tears in his eyes. His family was surprised; Mateo wasn't used to crying.

"What is it, Mateo?"

"It is a ticket to visit my friend in California. He sent me a ticket. I can't believe it! It works! It works! The visualization thing works! Mom, dad, I was visualizing myself traveling to California to see my mentor. For months I was visualizing it, and now it has become reality! This is so good!" And he ran to his parents and hugged them.

"Pedro," Mateo's mom added, "you better start visualizing lots of money to take your wife on a cruise to Europe."

Mateo's dad scratched his head and said, "I can try."

Everyone started laughing.

"Dad, mom, I can go, right?"

Mateo didn't know that his friend and mentor had already

called his parents to ask for permission to invite Mateo to California. His parents could feel the kind of person he was, and they also felt grateful that he was teaching Mateo about changing his mindset. They were watching Mateo improve his self-esteem and behavior. They were very proud, and they also felt a big change in their own way of thinking. Mateo was teaching his parents and little sister as he was studying; he was teaching his friends and even his teacher.

"Mateo, we know how important this is for you, and we feel that we can trust you. David already talked to us, and we know that you are going to be okay. He is a good person and so is his family. We already did our research. We are very proud of you."

That afternoon, Mateo went to his secret place in the mountains of Machu Picchu to meditate. He was so grateful. He loved meditating in this place. It was so magical; it was like the mountains were talking to him. This time, before starting his meditation, he said a prayer of gratitude. He felt so much love around him, and he felt a beautiful connection with infinite intelligence. The energy of this place was amazing.

Finally, the day came when Mateo was flying to America to see his mentor, who lives in California. Mateo couldn't sleep the night before, just thinking about his big day.

At the airport, Mateo's family was very enthusiastic about his trip, but his mom couldn't avoid feeling a little sad. This was the first time Mateo was going to be away from home. One month was too long for her, but she knew it was going to be a great experience for her son.

"Mateo, it's time for you to go through security. Make sure you have all your documents. David will be waiting for you at the airport gate in Los Angeles."

"Yes. It's time, mom and dad; I will miss you," and then he hugged them.

His mom couldn't avoid tearing up.

"It's ok, mom; I will be home soon! And I will bring you a beautiful present."

"I know you are going to be ok, Mateo. It's just that you are my sweet boy and, and …."

"It's ok, mom; I will be thinking about all of you."

"Mateo, please don't forget to call us when you get there, and remember that we are here for you," his father added.

"Yes, dad, I promise."

"Mateo, I love you, and I will miss you, but please bring me a nice dolly from California," his little sister asked.

"Lol, yes, my cute sis. I love you, family!" And Mateo left.

Mateo in California… The Adventure Begins

When the plane landed, Mateo was nervous to see his mentor. It had been over a year since he met him in Cusco, but since then, they had become more than friends. He was his best friend and mentor, and now they would be together again.

"I hope he remembers to pick me up," Mateo thought.

"Mateo, Mateo, over here!" Mateo turned around and saw David with a funny, decorated sign that said "Welcome to Los Angeles".

He rushed to him and gave him a big hug. "I can't believe I'm here with you. Thank you for all your help and for paying for this trip. This is a dream come true."

"You are very welcome! How was your flight, Mateo?"

"It was awesome! My seat was huge, comfortable, and retractable. I had my own tv, and a nice flight attendant was always taking care of me. I was nervous at the beginning of the flight, especially when it took off, but after that I was fine."

"I am so happy to hear that, Mateo; I remember my first flight, and I know what you mean. Are you ready for a learning experience? I am on vacation this month because I wanted to have time for you and our studies."

"Did you ask your boss for a vacation?" Mateo asked.

"No, Mateo, I am my own boss; I do my own schedule. This is a great way of living."

When approaching the exit at the airport, Mateo couldn't believe his eyes; a huge limousine was waiting for them.

"Is that limousine for us?"

"Of course! Peter, the chauffeur, will take us on a little tour around the city before going home. Is that okay with you?"

"David, this is amazing; yes, of course! I can't thank you enough for all this. Why are you doing all this for me?"

"Mateo," David replied, "you remind me a lot of myself. I was like you, hungry to learn more, and my mentor did the same for me. Now it's my turn; I know that one day, you will be able to do more for people. Life is about giving and receiving. Give with your heart, and receive gratefully; this is a law. There are so many more things to talk about. Mateo, this is just the beginning."

Mateo Meets David's Family

The following morning, after his arrival in California, Mateo woke up feeling great; he had never slept in such a huge bed and between so many cozy pillows. "Gosh!" He thought. "There are more pillows on just one bed than the total number of pillows in my house in Peru. This must be a dream."

He rushed to open the window and saw a beautiful backyard full of flowers and a huge swimming pool. "Wow…" He contemplated the view with amazement.

He gently opened the door, and a little, fluffy dog started to bark. He felt worried he may wake up the family.

"Hey, doggy, please don't bark; come on, doggy."

"Good morning, Mateo! Did you have a good sleep?"

"Good morning, David! Yes, thank you! Sorry I couldn't

stop the dog from barking."

"Lol. Don't worry," David replied, "he is just giving you a welcome bark."

"You have such an amazing home! It is huge! I felt lost in bed," Mateo commented.

David laughed, "I am glad that you are enjoying your stay here."

"I didn't want to wake you up so early. I thought you would be tired from your trip," David told Mateo.

"I was very tired last night when we arrived here, but I slept pretty well. I'm used to waking up very early. At home, I wake up around 5 am. I have to help my dad with the animals on the farm. We have cows, pigs, chickens, and ducks. It is hard work, but I love helping my dad."

"For sure you do, Mateo. You are very blessed to have a beautiful family that cares about you. Your parents are great people. I knew it right away when I talked to them on the phone. My grandparents took care of me when my parents died. They were nice to me, but many times, I felt lonely. I know they did the best they could, and I am grateful for them."

"Here she is… Hi, honey. I want you to meet Mateo. Mateo, this is my wife, Mia."

"Hi, Mateo! It is so nice to meet you finally. I have heard so many things about you. Sorry, I wanted to welcome you last night, but I came home after you went to bed."

Mateo felt so good around Mia. She had an angel face with beautiful red hair and big green eyes. He thought she was very tall, too.

"Nice to meet you! Thank you for having me in your home. You have an amazing home."

"Thank you, Mateo! Please let us know if you need anything. I'm sorry I have to fly to North Carolina for a couple of weeks. My aunt just passed, and I want to be there with my family."

"I am so sorry to hear that, Mrs. Mia."

"Please call me Mia, and thank you. I promise you, Mateo, when I come back, I will take you on a tour around my favorite places in California."

"Good morning, Daddy and Mommy."

"Hi, Ava! Honey, let me introduce you to a friend of ours named Mateo."

"Hi, Mateo. Nice to meet you. This is Eddy the Teddy. He says hi."

"Hi, Ava! Hi, Eddy the Teddy!"

"Do you play with dolls?" Ava asked.

Mateo smiled at her. "Yes, of course. I have a little sister whose name is Adela. We like to play with her Barbies. Also, we like to play hide and seek."

"Yes!!! I love hide and seek. Are you going to be here forever?" Ava asked Mateo.

"Ava, Mateo is going to be our guest for a month. I know you and Eddy the Teddy will make him feel welcome. This is the first time Mateo is away from his family," David told Ava.

"Yes, Daddy. I am very happy to have another brother!"

"We know, sweetheart," her mommy replied.

"There is one more member of the family, but he is at the University of Rhode Island, and I know you already met our fluffy Oreo."

"Yes, I did. He is very cute," Mateo replied.

"Well, let's have breakfast, and after that, I am going to take you to the nearby mall," David told Mateo.

Mateo wondered why David was going to take him to the mall. He was a little worried because he didn't bring much money. He saved all his salary and tips from his restaurant job back in Aguas Calientes, and he hoped it would be enough for the whole month.

The Secret of the Goal Card

"Our goals can only be reached through a vehicle of a plan, in which we must fervently believe and upon which we must vigorously act. There is no other route to success."

- Pablo Picasso

David and Mateo went to the mall that afternoon. They entered the teenage clothing section of a store, but Mateo felt a little uncomfortable as he was checking the price tags. He thought that was a lot of money to spend on clothes.

"Is there something wrong, Mateo? Is there something here that you like?" David asked.

"Well, everything looks nice, but I brought clothes; I don't think I need anything right now."

"Mateo, I asked you if there is something that you would

like to have, not something that you need; I want to buy it for you, whatever you need," David replied.

"I just don't want you to spend more money on me. You have already done so much for me, and I really appreciate it," Mateo answered David.

"I can feel your gratitude, but I really would like to buy you some clothes. Don't get me wrong; it's not because I don't like the clothes that you are wearing, but I saw your eyes when we entered the store; you wanted to have all of them until you saw the price tag."

"Wow, you have really good intuition; I feel that I can't keep any secrets from you," Mateo told David.

"Mateo, I invited you to my home, and you had to stop working to come here. You left your family, friends, and country. Plus, I want you to come to some of my seminars here in California. The attendees will wear corporate attire, and you are going to be my special guest."

"That is going to be super cool. If you put it that way, I accept you buying some clothes for me, but I need your help choosing what I need to wear. I have never worn such elegant clothing."

After shopping, Mateo and David went to a restaurant for lunch, and Mateo noticed something falling from David's pocket.

"David, this card fell from your pocket."

"Thank you, Mateo; this is my goal card."

"Your goal card?" Mateo asked.

"It is interesting how everything falls into place."

Mateo was wondering what his mentor was talking about.

"Yes, Mateo, this is the perfect time for one of the most important lessons for you. I wanted you to first learn about your creative faculties, or your GIFTS, before teaching you about the importance of a goal card. Now that you are more aware of the infinite potential that you have within yourself, it will be easier for you to imagine something great that you would love to enter your life."

Mateo felt the importance of what his mentor was about to teach him. He knew right away that it would change his life, and he listened to him, giving close and thoughtful attention.

"Mateo, many years ago, the man who changed my life completely, my best friend and mentor, sat down with me, and he gave me my very first goal card. He said to me, 'David, I want you to put your imagination in high gear, and I want you to write on this card what you would love to have; you do not need to know how you are going to get it or where the money or resources are going to come from. The only thing you need to know is that it is something that you really want.'"

David took a blank goal card and plastic sleeve out of his pocket; he put it on the table in front of Mateo, and looking squarely into Mateo's eyes, he continued…

"Mateo, it is important that you take some time for yourself and sit down and really think and ask yourself what you would love. Be honest with yourself; I want you to listen to YOU; you are in charge of your life. Think of what you want and write it on this card. Set a date that you are hoping your goal will be achieved by. Write it on the card, carry it in your pocket, and read it as often as possible every day. The repetition of reading the card is going to change your thinking, and with the repetition, you are going to get emotionally involved. If you stay emotionally involved with your goal, you are going to create an attractive force so powerful that you will attract your goal.

When you write your goal card, it MUST be in the present

tense. You can start with, 'I AM so happy and grateful now that I AM…' and keep repeating it. Do you know why people don't reach their goals? They keep it in the future. They think, 'I will be so happy and grateful when this happens.' If the date comes and you don't achieve your goal, just pick another date. Never change your goal; change your plans and change the date, but don't change your goal."

"David, do I have to carry my goal card in my pocket all the time?"

"Well, Mateo, my mentor suggested that I do that, and I've been doing it since then. You can carry it in your pocket or purse if you use one, or you can have it close to you all the time in a place where you can see it and touch it every day. Every time you touch the card, you activate cells in your brain that have the image of your goal. You wrote what you wanted on the card; that writing stirs your thoughts, and that's how the image gets impressed on those cells."

"Mateo, something very important to know is that you set goals not to achieve them, but to grow. That's why you have to be in love with your goal. If your goal is big enough, it is going to make you stretch, and sometimes you will feel uncomfortable. But because you are in love with your goal, you are going to keep going. It is going to make you change habits and patterns; you will change the way you are used to doing things. You are going to feel excited, but at the same time, you are going to face things that will scare you. That's why so many people don't reach their goals. They stop after the first obstacle."

"You are God's highest form of creation; no one knows what you are capable of doing. We don't want to stay where we are; we want to do better and make it bigger. If you know how to reach your goal or if you have already been there, then that is not a goal because you already know what to do. When you set your goal, you shouldn't have any idea how you will get there; but because you can see it in your mind and you act on it and believe it, you will be moving towards your goal, and it will move towards you.

Now, our goal is a mental seed. We don't know how long it will take for this goal to manifest. It is not like a physical seed that we plant and know when it's going to grow, so be patient. You will be tested, but if you keep studying these materials every day, you won't have any doubt that it will come. It is just a matter of time, Mateo."

Mateo took the card and sleeve and put it into his pocket, and looking into his mentor's eyes, he said, "I promise that I will carry this card in my pocket."

"I know you will, Mateo," David answered.

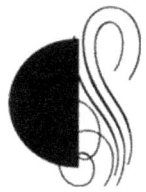

Mateo's Unforgettable First Seminar

A few days full of adventures and lessons had passed, and the day Mateo was waiting for had come. It was the day of his first seminar, and he was so proud that his mentor was the main speaker.

Mateo woke up very early on the day of the seminar; he was so happy but nervous at the same time. He showered, and he put on the clothes that his mentor had bought for him. He saw himself in the mirror and didn't recognize himself. He had a nice haircut and an elegant suit.

"Who is this guy? I need to take a picture of myself and show it to Ms.Rosita in Peru. She was always making fun of my messy hair."

Someone knocked at Mateo's door. "Can I come in?"

"Yes, Ava, please come in."

"Wow, you look so different! Daddy told me that you are going to his seminar today, and me and Eddy the Teddy wanted to say bye and good luck."

"Aww… that is very sweet, Ava. Thank you."

"Don't forget you promised to play hide and seek with me tomorrow. I can't wait to play with you again. It is so much fun!"

"You can count on that, and this time, I am not going to give up until I find you."

"Deal. I will see you later." And she left.

Someone else knocked on his door. "Good morning, Mateo! Can I come in?"

"Good morning, David. I'm ready; please come in."

"Wow, look at you; you look amazing!"

"Thank you, David! I'm very excited about the seminar. I don't even feel like having breakfast, which is weird for me to say."

"I understand; I remember my very first seminar. It was in Washington, and I was so nervous that I felt my legs shaking. However, you need to have a good breakfast in order to start your day, so I will see you at the table."

"Ok, I will be there soon."

After breakfast, as they were leaving the house and opening the front door, a huge black limousine was waiting for them outside. A nice gentleman opened the door for them. Mateo couldn't believe it.

"David, this is so awesome! I will never forget this moment; thank you for taking me to the seminar."

"Of course, Mateo; you are my special guest."

In the seminar, Mateo was introduced to so many people. His hands were sweating, so he didn't want to shake hands with anybody. But everyone was so nice and smiling that Mateo soon felt relaxed.

Mateo was sitting in the first row in front of the stage, and he was taking lots of notes on what his mentor was teaching.

He already studied the creative faculties… reason, intuition, imagination, memory, will, and perception, but his mentor went deeper into the subject, and there was so much more to learn. Mateo was fascinated by the way David conducted the seminar. When the lesson on attitude started, David approached Mateo at his table and introduced his friend to the audience.

"Now, I want you to meet a special guest at the seminar today. He came all the way from Peru and will stay at my house for a month as my guest; this boy is here because of his attitude. Since I met Mateo, he has had the perfect attitude, and he is studying these materials daily. Please, Mateo, stand up and tell everyone a little bit about yourself."

Mateo wasn't expecting David to introduce him to the audience, and at the beginning, he was shy. But as soon as he took the microphone, he couldn't stop talking and captivating the audience.

David was so proud of Mateo, like a father who is proud of his son. Mateo reminded David of himself when he was his age.

When the seminar was over, and they were on their way back home, David asked Mateo a question.

"During the seminar, how did you feel as you were talking in front of the audience?"

"At the beginning, I was so nervous, but something weird happened to me as soon as I took the microphone. It is hard to explain, but I felt more and more relaxed. Then I couldn't stop talking."

"I remember that part," David replied.

"Did I talk too much?" Mateo asked David.

"I'm just kidding; you were perfect. They loved you, and you know why?" David asked Mateo.

"Not really," Mateo replied.

"Because you talked from your heart and expressed yourself; you are proud of who you are and where you come from, and you should be. That's why they loved you. Always be YOU, Mateo."

"My grandpa used to tell me to be myself all the time. I will never forget that."

"Your grandpa was very wise to tell you that."

"He passed away when I was 7. He was my best friend; I will never forget him, and I miss him so much." Mateo told David.

"Sorry to hear that, Mateo, but you can talk to him; we are energy, and energy never dies. Remember, the spirit is 100% evenly present in all places at the same time. Talk to him; tell him how much you love him and miss him. He won't be able to answer back, but you will feel him."

Mateo smiled at his mentor and promised him that he would do it.

Healing Mateo's Heart

"Your worst enemy cannot harm you as much as your own unguarded thoughts."

- Buddha

Two weeks had passed since Mateo arrived in California, and Mia, David's wife, came back from her trip to North Carolina. She brought gifts for everybody, and Mateo was happy to see her. David and Mia planned to take Mateo and Ava to their beach house for the weekend. Mateo and Ava were excited. They became very good friends, and Mateo felt at home. Although he missed his family back in Peru, he would never forget David and his family.

"Mateo, you can't catch me!" Ava yelled.

"Just wait and see," Mateo replied.

"Kids! Food is ready!" Mia called.

They were playing in the sand with Oreo, Ava's dog.

"We are coming!" Mateo yelled.

After the perfect lunch together, full of laughter and stories, David and Mateo planned to ride their bikes around the boulevard. The weather was perfect, the sky was blue, and there were not many people around the boulevard.

"Mateo, you can ride my son's bicycle; it is the perfect height for you."

"Thank you, David; I promise to take care of his bike."

"Of course," David answered.

Mateo loved riding bikes around the boulevard. He felt the air touching his face. A feeling of joy and freedom surrounded his body. He was pedaling quickly to reach David, and later, he passed him. Mateo turned back to him and yelled, "You can't catch me!" David laughed at him and said, "Just wait and see." David started pedaling even faster, when suddenly, he lost control of his bike and fell to the ground. Mateo rushed to him and started screaming, "Are you ok, David? Are you ok? Please say something."

"I am ok, Mateo; please calm down," David told him.

"I'm so sorry, David; it's all my fault."

"Hey, boy! It's all good! It's not your fault; it's nobody's fault; I just didn't see that rock ahead of me."

David touched Mateo's hand, and he felt his hands shaking. He asked, "Why are you so scared?"

Mateo looked at David and couldn't stop crying. David knew there was something in Mateo that needed to be healed.

David asked Mateo to breathe deeply in and out for a couple of minutes and then asked, "Are you feeling better, Mateo?"

"Yes, thank you, David."

"Let's go home. I am getting hungry, and I would like to show you my special place to see the sunset," David told Mateo.

Mateo was quiet after the incident on the boulevard. He looked sad, and David wasn't used to seeing him like that.

Back at the beach house, David invited Mateo to go for a walk to his favorite place on the beach to view the sunset. It was an incredible view with a sense of peace in the air. They sat on the sand and didn't say a word to each other for some time.

"Mateo, I want you to know that I am here for you. And if something is bothering you or makes you feel sad or frustrated, you can count on me and tell me whatever is in your heart whenever you are ready."

Mateo kept silent, and suddenly he started to talk… "If I didn't scare him with that stupid joke, he would be alive."

David stared at Mateo and asked him. "Who is that, Mateo? You can tell me."

"Papa Alejandro, my grandpa; I used to call him Papa."

Mateo told David that one day, he and Grandpa Alejandro were riding their bikes home on the way back from his school. Suddenly, he screamed when he saw a chicken in front of him, and he immediately pressed the brakes. The chicken ran away, but Mateo's grandpa, who was riding behind him, jumped off of his bike and landed on his back. Mateo told David that he ran to his grandpa crying and that his grandpa looked at him and asked him why he was crying. He told him that he was okay and that he just had a little bruise. However, the ambulance had to come to carry him because he couldn't move. He was 86 and was a very strong, old man, but he couldn't recover after that fall.

"After that day, I took care of Papa Alejandro. He wasn't

able to move around so much anymore, but he never complained. One day, I came back from school and found out that my grandpa was in the hospital. My mom told me that he got pneumonia and he was very sick. After a few more days, he died at the hospital. I will never forget that. I felt lost, but my family and friends showed me so much love that I started to feel better again. But I will never forget him."

"Mateo, I can tell that you are holding on to negative feelings about what happened to your grandpa. You somehow feel responsible for his death, and that is a terrible feeling."

"Guilt is a powerful, negative emotion; you have to free yourself from what happened in the past. Mateo, we only have this moment. We don't know how much time we have left, and spending your time focusing on the past is to waste the only thing that we have, which is this moment. I want you to look around you right now."

Mateo looked at the amazing sunset ahead of them.

"God is giving you the opportunity to enjoy the gift of life. Why do you want to waste your time reliving negative emotions? It is time to let it go. I can't do it for you, Mateo. I can help you, and I will, but you have to do it for yourself."

"I know, David, but it still hurts so much. Why do bad things have to happen?"

"I don't know why bad things happen. We can't do anything about the situation, but what we can do is change our perception of the situation and how we respond to it. Only God knows why it happened, and I believe that in this world, everything happens for a reason. It is sometimes not easy to accept that, but everything in this world operates by law.

Mateo, you want to grow in awareness, and let me tell you that I've learned more from my negative experiences than my positive ones. Very bad things have happened to me, that if I tell you, I will spoil your day. But those experiences were necessary for me to grow, transform me into the person that I am now, and help me to teach others. If you are holding onto something that is not serving you, it will hinder your growth."

Mateo knew the powerful truth of his mentor's words. He felt comforted, and he knew he would need help in letting go of that feeling from the past that was deep inside of him.

"David, can you teach me how to let go of things and how to heal my heart from memories from the past?" Mateo asked.

"Sure, Mateo. I am going to give you an affirmation that will help you release resentment and guilt. I want you to write it down, memorize it, and whenever you feel guilt or resentment again, I want you to say it out loud in front of the mirror and look into your eyes. Your eyes are the windows to your soul. Do it with feeling, and keep doing it until you feel better. If the feelings come back, do it again. If you can't be in front of a mirror, do it wherever you are, but it is important that you add feeling to it. Now write down the following…"

"I willingly release the thoughts and things that have cluttered my mind.

I release… (Insert the name of the person you hold resentment for; you can write your name here.)

To their highest good, happiness, health, wealth, and peace of mind."

"Do it with feeling, and you will see how effective it is," David suggested to Mateo.

"Thanks, David. I already feel much better. I didn't see my past experience from that point of view. I think I have to go back to studying my GIFTS and focus on perception," Mateo told David.

"That is a great idea. You always want to keep studying. Even if you memorized it, repetition is the key to changing your programming."

A Morning Practice That Will Change Mateo's Life

The next morning, David was pleased to see Mateo happy again, with a big smile and sparkling eyes. The whole family was having breakfast on the balcony facing the ocean. Mateo was telling silly jokes and making everyone laugh. Fluffy Oreo was under the table, waiting for someone's crumbs to fall. Everyone was having a great time. After breakfast, David called Mateo to his studio for a lesson.

Mateo entered the studio without knowing he was about to receive one of the most important lessons of his life…

"Mateo, sit down and pay close attention to what I am about to tell you."

Mateo took his notebook and pen, ready to start taking notes and paying attention to David.

"Mateo, as I told you before, everything in this world

operates by law. Sometimes you may feel that everything in your life is going wrong, and sometimes you will feel that your life is going perfectly smoothly. There is a law of rhythm. If you understand this law, you will realize that you won't feel great all the time; there are times that you will feel down, and that's perfectly normal. There are good times and bad times, but if you keep a good attitude, the low swing will change very fast. And if you study the laws of the universe, you will know that the low swing will change soon."

"I have an exercise that my mentor gave me many years ago. I was going through a difficult situation, and I asked him for help. He took his pen and told me to write down 10 things in my life that I was grateful for at that moment. He told me that I was focusing on the wrong things that were happening to me and that many good things were happening in my life. Then he said that after making my list, I should send love to 3 people that were hurting me or bothering me, and that if I didn't have anyone that was bothering me, I could send love to myself. After that, I should be quiet for a few minutes and ask the spirit for guidance.

I have been using that formula since then, and let me tell you, it works like magic. If you have a problem sending love to someone that is bothering you, you can try this small trick that I use. I think about someone that I love, connect with those feelings, gently push the image off of them, and slowly replace it with the image of the person that I want to send love to. This makes it easier. During my teaching career, I was able to help many people using this technique. I would suggest you use it. You will be surprised."

"I promise you, I will use it, especially in my downswings. There is this kid in school that likes to make fun of me. He calls me 'Dumbo Ears'. It really bothers me. I will start sending him love."

"Good, Mateo. I would suggest you start your morning with this practice. If you start your day with gratitude, your day will be amazing."

"What is your morning routine?" Mateo asked David.

"That is a good question, Mateo; I have a morning ritual. When I wake up, I like to say a small prayer first. I thank God for the new day, and I ask him to somehow let me serve during the day. We can serve others in many ways; even a nice smile to someone on the street is a good way of serving others. There are many people out there who need our smile. Then, I wash up and go to my studio. The first thing I do there is touch my goal card, think about my goal, and write my goal out. Then I do my gratitude exercise that I just showed you, and I meditate for 15 minutes."

"David, do you listen to a meditation song when you meditate?"

"Sometimes; it depends on how my spirit feels. What I like to do when I meditate is to imagine a beautiful light going around my body, and that light is making me whole and perfect. I see myself in perfect health, and I also visualize my goal. I feel so much gratitude when I meditate. It's a beautiful feeling and a perfect way to start your day. Do what makes you feel good. That is the key. If you feel that it is getting automatic without feelings, change it a little bit from time to time. My mentor told me once that it's not about how you spend your day, but how you start your day. And I will never forget that.

After my meditation, I study for one hour or more, depending on my schedule; studying is a habit for me. If you turn study into a habit, you will change your whole world to overall success. A habit is something we do without any conscious thought. I would suggest you do the same, Mateo."

Mateo enjoyed the moments he spent with his mentor, the teaching, and the new learning. He was going to miss it so much.

"Ok, Mateo, let's get ready to go to the movies. Mia and Ava will be ready soon."

Mateo Discovers His Purpose in Life

"I dream my painting, and then I paint my dream."

- Van Gogh

The day of the last seminar on Mateo's trip had arrived, and Mia, David's wife, was joining them. Before the seminar started, some people who had attended the previous seminar approached Mateo to welcome him and express their friendship. Mateo felt the beautiful energy in the air. He felt so much gratitude for all the nice people he had met on his trip. He had learned so many lessons and was ready to implement them into his daily life. Suddenly, his thoughts were interrupted by an announcement from David on the stage. Everyone was standing up and clapping for him. David looked amazing and captivated the audience. As soon as he started teaching, everyone started taking notes…

"I want you to project yourself about 3 to 5 years or more into the future. What is the ideal life for you? Just let your imagination flow, and do not give any attention to your circumstances. How do you see yourself living? Maybe you want a lake house or many houses; maybe you want to live in Europe or America or have a luxury car. How do you want to live? Your VISION is a long-range view of a multiplicity of things that you want to do. We studied our GIFTS, our created faculties. Use them to create your vision. Use your IMAGINATION to create it, hold it with your WILL, and write it down. As I told you, before writing, stir your thoughts, and visualize them in your spare time. Remember, your VISION is not a goal. Your GOALS are stepping stones to reach your vision and purpose.

Your life PURPOSE is your reason for living; your purpose will kick you out of bed in the morning; it's why you are living. You feel passionate about it, and it's like the fuel for living. There are a lot of people that don't know their purpose. In order to find your purpose, I would suggest you sit down and be relaxed, preferably in the early morning, and have a pen and pad with you. Ask yourself, 'If I could do what I love every day all day, what would it be?' And write down whatever comes to your mind. Do it often, and don't force yourself; just relax; it will come to you. Maybe it will take some time, a few days or months, but if you do this practice often, it will come, and you will know it. Your purpose is what you absolutely love doing."

David approached Mateo, who was sitting at a table close to the stage. He looked at him and said, "Find your purpose, and then make the decision to dedicate your life to your purpose."

Something clicked inside Mateo. It was like an intuitive hit, and he got so excited at that moment that he wanted to jump for joy; his heart started to beat faster, and for some strange reason, he had tears in his eyes. He couldn't wait to be alone with his mentor and tell him his purpose. He felt that his life had changed at that very moment.

After the seminar, Mia and Mateo went home. David had to stay longer because of a meeting with his team. Mateo was waiting impatiently for his mentor to arrive home. He had so much to tell him.

Finally, David arrived. It was late at night, but Mateo was awake. He stood by the front door and unintentionally scared his mentor.

"I'm so glad you are here; I was waiting for you."

"Hi Mateo, why are you up so late? Are you feeling okay?" David asked.

"Better than ever; I wanted to talk to you. I promise not to take too much of your time. I know you are very tired."

David was really wondering what Mateo had to tell him that he couldn't wait until the next day.

"Sure, Mateo, just give me a few minutes, and I will be in my studio."

"Sure," Mateo replied.

"Ok, Mateo, I am intrigued; what is so important that you want to tell me?"

"David, I know my purpose in life!" David looked into Mateo's eyes.

"You do?"

"Yes! I got an intuitive hit in the seminar today. David, I want to do what you are doing; I want to be a motivational speaker!"

David approached him and asked him, "Why do you want to be a motivational speaker?"

"I loved talking in front of a big audience in your previous seminar. It felt so good. But the most important reason is because I'm in love with these materials, and I feel different. My life has changed so much since I started studying them. The proof is that I am here with you right now, in your home. I want to be able to teach this material to as many people as I can and change their lives."

David looked at Mateo with pride and said, "Mateo, you just reminded me of the day I found my purpose in life; I did the same as you just did. I told my mentor, and I couldn't wait to tell him. I am very happy for you. I didn't tell you, but the night before I met you in Peru, I had a dream of my mentor. And in my dream, he told me to follow my heart.

Then, when I met you, I felt a strong connection with you. It was like I knew you before. I do believe in past lives, and I believe we met before. Mateo, I exercise my intuition so much that I can sense people's aura, and I make decisions based on my intuition. That's why you are here with me. I followed my heart. I saw in your eyes that you wanted to know more and to be more. You are eager to learn and change. If you keep studying and following your heart, I know that you are going to be a great speaker one day."

Mateo felt so uplifted as he listened to his mentor. He could see himself teaching to an audience, and he was determined to do that.

"But I am going to tell you something very important. Mateo, you are going to be tested. There are going to be times when you may want to quit. To be in front of an audience is not an easy thing to do. You have to study a lot and be able to answer different questions. You will have doctors, engineers, philosophers, and different people with different backgrounds in front of you, and if you are not prepared to answer properly, they will never come back. And soon, your reputation will go downhill. I am not trying to scare you; I know if I can do it, you can do it too. But I want you to know that if you really want something, you have to go for it and take it."

Mateo stood up from his chair, looked into his mentor's eyes, and said, "David, I promise you that I will be one of the best motivational speakers of all time. I know it is my purpose, I can feel it, and I will do whatever is required in order to get there."

David put his hand on Mateo's shoulder and told him, "I know you will, Mateo. I know you will."

An Unforgettable Trip is Coming to an End

It was Tuesday night, five days before Mateo's trip back to Peru. He tossed from one side of his bed to the other. He turned on the lamp and touched the picture of his family in Peru that was on top of his nightstand. He smiled and thought that soon, he would be there. He missed them so much, even though he talked with them on the phone every day; it was not enough. But at the same time, he started to get sad, realizing that soon he would be far from David and his family. "Why does it have to be like this?" he asked himself. Then suddenly, the word "perception" came to his mind. Ah, I know; I should shift my perception about this situation. He took a pad and pen and started to write down all the things that he was grateful for. He felt so blessed to be having that experience, to meet David in Peru and become good friends, more than friends. He found his mentor and best friend, was staying at his home, and had met his family. That was something that he would never forget and always be thankful for. His gratitude list was long, and finally, Mateo was able to fall asleep with a nice feeling in his heart.

In the morning, the family was at the kitchen table organizing Mateo's farewell party. They wanted to throw him a surprise party with all the friends he had made in California. When Mateo entered the kitchen for some milk, the family changed the conversation, and Mateo discerned that something was going on.

"Good morning. Is everything ok?" Mateo asked them.

"Good morning, Mateo. Today is a beautiful day, and we are just planning our day," Mia answered Mateo.

"Come and sit with us, Mateo; I made your favorite breakfast," David requested.

"Yummy strawberry pancakes! I love them; I will eat them all."

"Mateo, do you remember Mr. Stewart from the seminar? He is a tall, bald guy. He was wearing a light blue suit at the last seminar." David told Mateo.

"Yes, I was talking with him and his wife. They are very funny; they like to tell jokes." Mateo answered.

"Yes, they are a very nice couple; we have known them since Ava was born. He is a prominent doctor, and his wife is the principal of Ava's elementary school." Mia replied.

"Well, get your swimming suit and sun lotion ready; they invited us to go on a fishing trip on his boat. Do you know how to fish, Mateo?"

"I'm not an expert, but Grandpa Alejandro and I used to go to the river and catch trout. I really enjoyed it. Then we would go home, fry them, and eat them with coffee, fresh bread, and Criolla salsa, which is a preparation of red onions, lime juice, aji amarillo peppers, cilantro, salt, and pepper. It is so good!"

"That sounds delicious," Mia said.

"I have a great idea," David added.

"You should teach us how to prepare Criolla salsa tomorrow. We can have a Peruvian-style dinner with the fish we catch. What do you think, Mateo?"

"I'm on it!" Mateo exclaimed.

On the day of the fishing trip, everyone had a great time. Mr. Stewart and his family were happy to host the trip. They told jokes, and Mateo caught some big fish. He loved Mr. Stewart's boat; it was luxurious, very big, and had a slide. Mr. Stewart's son Paul, who was 13, sat next to Mateo and watched as he was fishing. He was amazed to see how many fish Mateo was catching.

Back at Mr. Stewart's home, Mateo taught them how to prepare Peruvian Criolla salsa. They had some fresh baguettes and coffee ready. David recorded a video of Mateo's cooking lessons. He thought about how much he had learned from him. Mateo was like a little, pure-hearted kid. He knew he would miss his Peruvian friend. After the dinner, everyone complimented Mateo for the great Peruvian-style, fried fish they had just enjoyed. Mateo felt proud and happy that he was able to share a traditional way of eating fried fish in his country.

On Friday morning, everything was prepared for Mateo's surprise farewell party. The plan was that after breakfast, Mia would take Mateo to the mall while the others finished decorating the house. Their friends would arrive around 4 pm.

"Mateo, since you are leaving on Sunday morning, I need you to come with me to the mall after breakfast. I want to buy some souvenirs for your family in Peru. Can you do that for me? I don't know what to buy for them, and after that, I will take you to my favorite place in town for lunch. It is a fancy restaurant." Mia told Mateo.

"I would love that! Thank you for thinking about my family. They will be very happy," Mateo replied.

At 4:30 pm, Mia and Mateo came back from lunch with bags full of presents. Mateo came with just one small suitcase and would return to Peru with 4 big suitcases. He planned to get ready for his trip later in the afternoon.

When they got home, Mateo noticed a lot of cars parked close to the house and thought, "Someone must be having a party." As they entered the home, they dropped the shopping bags on the floor, and Mia asked Matteo to go with her to the backyard. She told Mateo that she wanted an opinion about some flowers she had bought.

Mateo realized that the windows were closed, and everything looked dark inside the house. He wasn't used to seeing the house so dark. Their windows were always open, and sunlight came into the house most of the time, with a beautiful view of the backyard and pool. When Mateo opened the door to the backyard, everyone yelled out loud, "Surprise!" David, his family, and his new friends in California were there; everything was decorated with beautiful colored balloons, banners, and pictures, and there was a cake and lots of food. He couldn't believe his friends were having a surprise party for him. He felt so happy and emotional.

During the party, everyone had a great time. Mateo danced with Ava in the middle of the dance floor with all his friends around them. Suddenly, the music stopped, and David and Mia approached Mateo with a big box that had a beautiful, green ribbon.

"Mateo, this is a gift from me and my family; I know you are going to like it," David told Mateo.

"Mateo, we are going to miss you," Mia added.

"Wow! This is a big box!" Mateo wondered why the box had holes in it.

"You already gave me so many surprises. I love surprises. Thank you so much!"

"Open the box, Mateo!" Ava yelled.

David placed the box on a table next to Mateo, and suddenly, the box started to move.

"Oh, a moving box!" Mateo exclaimed, and everybody laughed. Mateo proceeded to open the box carefully, and a cute, little puppy started to bark.

"I can't believe it's a puppy! A cute, little, fluffy puppy!"

Mateo hugged the puppy and started to cry. "This is the best gift ever. I have always wanted a puppy. He is spotted like Milo. I think I am going to name him Milo because he looks like him. Thank you so much! I wish I had something for you," Mateo told the family.

"Your presence is enough of a gift for us; I am happy you like Milo; he is very friendly and playful," David told Mateo.

At the end of the party, everyone took pictures with Mateo and Milo and wished them a safe return home. Mateo felt tired. It was a long day for him, but he felt so happy at the same time. He had mixed feelings. He was happy he was going back to his family and country, but at the same time, he was going to miss his new friends in California.

At 7 am on Sunday morning, the family took Mateo to the airport. He had 5 big suitcases to take back to Peru, and he traveled with Milo inside the cabin. He flew in first class, and he was hoping that Milo would feel good inside the airplane. He was a small toy poodle, but he liked to bark a lot. When the time came to say goodbye, Mateo felt very sad. Little Ava hugged him and started to cry.

"Please promise me that you are going to come back soon; we haven't finished the big Barbie puzzle yet."

Mateo teared up while looking at Ava and told her, "I promise you I will, and I will call you very often."

Then, Mia hugged Mateo and told him, "You are going to be missed. Have a safe trip, Mateo."

"I will miss you too, Mia; thank you for everything."

Mateo looked at David and hugged him. "I've been using my GIFTS since you taught me about them. I am getting good at them, especially with memory. My teachers in Peru are going to be amazed, but there is one gift that I have difficulty with, especially in moments like this. Do you know which one I'm talking about, David?"

David looked at Mateo and smiled at him. "Perception is not an easy creative faculty to master, but it is possible if you continue to practice changing your perception in your favor. You are going to be with your family in Peru soon, and you are going to be happy again. I understand your feelings. It's part of growing. I will call you often, and you promise to call me whenever you want. If I don't answer, it is because I am in a meeting or traveling, but I will call you back. Now, let me see a smile on your face."

Mateo looked at him and smiled.

"This is the Mateo I know, always smiling. Don't you dare lose your smile. I love you, Mateo; you are like my son. I will be thinking about you. Remember, we are all connected. Have a safe trip." Then Mateo left.

After boarding the plane, he sat in his seat, petting Milo, and looked through the window. He said to himself, "David, I now know my purpose in life, and I won't stop studying. It's time for me to implement everything you taught me and be the person I was meant to be. I am flying home today, but Mateo will be back soon. It's a promise."

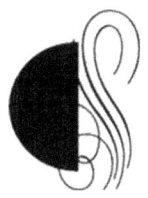

About the Author

Sara D'Ambrosio is passionate about helping people reach their full potential. She is the author of the **Bluely the Happy Blue Bird** *series, a collection of educational children's books that teach children about self-esteem, positive thinking, and imagination. She is the co-author of an upcoming book – Learning Through Pain. She is also a certified life coach who helps adults and children harness the power of their mindset.*

Sara is driven by her passion to make a difference in the world, and she is determined to continue helping people reach their full potential.

Contact Sara: *If you would like information about Sara's coaching programs or coaching for kids and adults, please send her an email at* saradambrosiomastermind@gmail.com

or visit her website at

https://www.saradambrosiomastermind.com/

www.ingramcontent.com/pod-product-compliance
Lightning Source LLC
Chambersburg PA
CBHW060840050426
42453CB00008B/761